W9-ASB-855

CONTENTS

LAKE CLASSICS

*Great British and Irish
Short Stories I*

E. M.
FORSTER

Stories retold by Joanne Suter
Illustrated by James McConnell

LAKE EDUCATION
Belmont, California

LAKE CLASSICS

Great American Short Stories I

Washington Irving, Nathaniel Hawthorne, Mark Twain, Bret Harte, Edgar Allan Poe, Kate Chopin, Willa Cather, Sarah Orne Jewett, Sherwood Anderson, Charles W. Chesnutt

Great American Short Stories II

Herman Melville, Stephen Crane, Ambrose Bierce, Jack London, Edith Wharton, Charlotte Perkins Gilman, Frank R. Stockton, Hamlin Garland, O. Henry, Richard Harding Davis

Great British and Irish Short Stories I

Arthur Conan Doyle, Saki (H. H. Munro), Rudyard Kipling, Katherine Mansfield, Thomas Hardy, E. M. Forster, Robert Louis Stevenson, H. G. Wells, John Galsworthy, James Joyce

Great Short Stories from Around the World I

Guy de Maupassant, Anton Chekhov, Leo Tolstoy, Selma Lagerlöf, Alphonse Daudet, Mori Ogwai, Leopoldo Alas, Rabindranath Tagore, Fyodor Dostoevsky, Honoré de Balzac

Cover and Text Designer: Diann Abbott

Copyright © 1994 by Lake Education, a division of Lake Publishing Company, 500 Harbor Blvd., Belmont, CA 94002. All rights reserved. No part of this book may be reproduced by any means, transmitted, or translated into a machine language without written permission from the publisher.

Library of Congress Catalog Number: 94-075356
ISBN 1-56103-031-7
Printed in the United States of America
1 9 8 7 6 5 4 3 2

❦ Lake Classic Short Stories ❧

"The universe is made of stories, not atoms."
—Muriel Rukeyser

"The story's about you."
—Horace

Everyone loves a good story. It is hard to think of a friendlier introduction to classic literature. For one thing, short stories are *short*—quick to get into and easy to finish. Of all the literary forms, the short story is the least intimidating and the most approachable.

Great literature is an important part of our human heritage. In the belief that this heritage belongs to everyone, *Lake Classic Short Stories* are adapted for today's readers. Lengthy sentences and paragraphs are shortened. Archaic words are replaced. Modern punctuation and spellings are used. Many of the longer stories are abridged. In all the stories, painstaking care has been taken to preserve the author's unique voice.

Lake Classic Short Stories have something for everyone. The hundreds of stories in the collection cover a broad terrain of themes, story types, and styles. Literary merit was a deciding factor in story selection. But no story was included unless it was as enjoyable as it was instructive. And special priority was given to stories that shine light on the human condition.

Each book in the *Lake Classic Short Stories* is devoted to the work of a single author. Little-known stories of merit are included with famous old favorites. Taken as a whole, the collected authors and stories make up a rich and diverse sampler of the story-teller's art.

Lake Classic Short Stories guarantee a great reading experience. Readers who look for common interests, concerns, and experiences are sure to find them. Readers who bring their own gifts of perception and appreciation to the stories will be doubly rewarded.

❦ E. M. Forster ❧
(1879–1970)

About the Author

Edward Morgan Forster was born in London. His father died before the boy turned two, and his mother raised him alone. She would remain his loving companion until her death in 1945.

Because he was a day student at a boarding school, Forster had an unhappy time in the English public schools. But his college years at Cambridge were much happier. There, he met people like himself who were interested in literature and art.

In the following years, these new friends would become known as the "Bloomsbury Group." These were artists and writers who met regularly in the Bloomsbury section of London.

Forster had found his home in this group of talented people. Including

Forster, they all became famous as artistic and intellectual leaders before, during, and after World War I.

When Forster was 22, he visited Greece and Italy. This trip had an influence on him that lasted for the rest of his life. He saw Greek and Italian peasant life as colorful and free. In contrast, middle-class English life seemed stuffy indeed. But Forster was a great admirer of English literature. He once wrote, "English literature is a flying fish. It is a sample of the life that goes on day after day beneath the surface."

Forster's visit to India when he was 33 had a deep effect on him. Twelve years after that visit, he wrote his greatest novel, *A Passage to India*. This famous story deals with the problems caused by British rule in India. It was made into a movie in 1984.

Forster once defined the short story as "a chopped-off length of the tapeworm of time." Read on, for a few samples of Forster's view of the tapeworm of time.

The Story of a Panic

Wouldn't *anyone* enjoy a summer holiday in Italy? Young Eustace is grumpy and bored—until he goes along on a picnic in the mountains. After that his whole life is changed. What happened that day in the chestnut woods?

"IT LOOKS AS IF YOU HAD A VISIT FROM SOME GOATS."

The Story of a Panic

I

Eustace's new life certainly began that afternoon. It happened in the chestnut woods above the town of Ravello.

I must tell you at once that I am a plain and simple man. I do not pretend to be a great writer. Still, I can tell a story just as it happened. I have, therefore, decided to describe the surprising things that went on eight years ago.

Ravello is a delightful place. It has a

delightful little hotel in which we met some charming people. There were the two Miss Robinsons. They had been there for six weeks with Eustace, their nephew. Eustace was then just a boy. He was about 14 years old.

Mr. Sandbach had also been there some time. Once he had been an officer of a church in the north of England. But then he had left his job because of bad health. At Ravello, he had taken charge of Eustace's schooling—which had been quite poor. Mr. Sandbach was hoping to prepare Eustace for one of our great public schools.

Then there was Mr. Leyland, a would-be artist. Finally, there was the nice landlady, Signora Scafetti. Usually the hotel had a pleasant, English-speaking waiter named Emmanuele. But, at the time of which I am speaking, Emmanuele was away visiting his sick father.

To this circle I add myself, my wife, and my two daughters. I liked most of the company well enough. But there were two of them who I did not enjoy at all. One was the artist, Leyland. The other was Eustace, the nephew of the two Miss Robinsons.

Leyland thought too highly of himself. That will be clear to you later in my story. I need not go on about it here. But Eustace was something else. It is impossible to describe how people disliked him.

I like boys, as a rule, and I tried to be friendly. My daughters and I invited him out. "No, walking is such a bore," he said. Then I asked him to come for a swim. "No, I cannot swim," he said.

"Every English boy should be able to swim," I said. "I will teach you myself."

"There, Eustace dear!" said Miss Robinson. "Here is a chance for you."

But he said he was afraid of the water! A boy—afraid! But, of course, I said no more about the matter.

I would not have minded so much if he had been a bookworm. But he neither played hard nor worked hard. He liked to pass time resting in an easy chair. Sometimes he wandered along the road with his feet kicking up dust and his shoulders stooping forward.

Of course, his skin was pale and his chest was thin. He had little muscle. His aunts thought he must be treated carefully. But what he really needed was a firm hand.

Then came the day that no one will ever forget. We all prepared to go up in the chestnut woods for a picnic. Only my daughter Janet stayed behind. She wanted to finish her watercolor painting. It was not a very good one, I am afraid.

There is a reason for wandering off into these unimportant facts. In my mind, I cannot separate them from the rest of the day. It is the same with our talk during the picnic. Everything is mixed together in my brain. I recall that we headed up the hill for about two hours. Then we left the donkeys that carried the two Miss Robinsons and my wife. From there we all climbed on foot to the head of the valley.

Of course, I have visited many fine places before and since. But I have never found a place that pleased me more than this spot. The valley ended in a great hollow, shaped like a cup. The canyons and the hills all around the valley were covered with leafy chestnut trees. The scene looked like a many-fingered green hand, turned upwards and holding us in its grasp. Far down the valley, we could see Ravello and the sea. That was the only sign of another world.

"Oh, what a perfectly lovely place!" said my daughter Rose. "What a picture it would make!"

"Yes," said Mr. Sandbach. "Many an art

gallery would be proud to have a painting half as beautiful as this."

"Oh, no," said Leyland, the would-be artist. "This scene would make a very poor picture. Indeed, it is not suited for painting at all."

"And why is that?" said Rose. She spoke to him with respect—as if he knew what he was talking about.

"In the first place," he answered, "look how plain and straight the line of the hill is against the sky. It would need breaking up. And look at where we are standing. The whole thing is wrong. Besides, the colors are too much the same."

"I do not know much about pictures," I put in. "I do not pretend to know. But I know what is beautiful when I see it. I am most happy with this."

"Indeed, who could help being happy!" said the older Miss Robinson. Mr. Sandbach said the same.

"Ah!" said Leyland. "Of course, a person with a paint brush looks at nature quite differently than the person with a camera."

Poor Rose had brought her camera along with her. I was worried that Mr. Leyland might have hurt her feelings. But I did not want to argue, so I just turned away. I helped my wife and Miss Mary Robinson put out the picnic lunch. I'm afraid it was not much of a lunch.

"Eustace, dear," said his aunt, "come and help us."

He was in a very bad mood that morning. As usual, he had not wanted to come. His aunts had nearly let him stay at the hotel. There he would have surely spent the day bothering Janet. But I, after checking with the aunts, spoke to him rather sharply about the need for exercise. So Eustace had come along. But he was even more difficult than usual.

Doing as he was told was not the boy's

strong point. He always questioned every order. When he obeyed, he only did so unhappily. I would hope that any son of mine would do as I asked, quickly and cheerfully.

"I'm—coming—Aunt—Mary," Eustace answered at last. He was hanging back, cutting a piece of wood to make a whistle. He took care not to arrive until we had finished.

"Well, well, sir!" said I. "You finally come over at the end and find the work all done."

He sighed, for he could not stand being teased. Miss Mary handed him the wing of the chicken. I felt he hadn't earned it, so I tried to stop her. It made me angry to think that we weren't enjoying the sun and the woods. Instead we were all worrying over a spoiled boy.

After lunch, he was a little less of a bother. He went off to sit under a tree trunk and go on carving his whistle. I was glad to see him busy for once. We sat back and looked at the scenery.

Those sweet chestnut trees of the South are not much compared to our bigger Northern trees. Still, they clothed the hills and valleys in a most pleasing way. Only two clearings broke the covering of trees. We were sitting in one of them.

Because the few trees around us had all been cut down, Leyland began to complain about the landowner.

"All the poetry is going from nature," he cried. "Her lakes are drained. Her forests are cut down. Everywhere we see the ruin spreading!"

I have owned some land myself. I answered that *some* cutting was needed to make room for the larger trees. Besides, a landowner has a right to earn something from his lands.

"To me, the thought that a tree should be turned into money is sickening," said Leyland.

"I don't agree," I replied politely. "I see

no reason to refuse the gifts of nature because they have cash value."

This did not stop him. "It is no matter," the would-be artist went on. "We are all hopeless! It is because of us that the spirits have left the streams and the mountains. Remember Pan, the Greek god of the forests? The Greeks of old described him as part man, part goat. It is because of us that Pan no longer makes his home in our woods."

"Pan!" cried Mr. Sandbach. His deep voice filled the valley as if it were a great green church. "Pan is dead. That is why the woods do not house him." Then he began to tell a story about sailors who were sailing near the coast. Three times, as the story went, they heard a loud voice saying, "The great god Pan is dead."

"Yes. The great god Pan is dead," said Leyland. Then he pretended to be overcome with silent sorrow— as artists are so likely to do. But his cigar went out, and he had to ask me for a match.

"How very interesting," said Rose. "I do wish I knew some history."

"It is not worth your notice," said Mr. Sandbach. "Eh, Eustace?"

Eustace was finishing his whistle. He looked up. He frowned in that ugly way that his aunts let him get away with. He did not answer.

The talk went on about this and about that. Then it died out. It was a bright afternoon in May. The light green of the young chestnut leaves was pretty against the dark blue of the sky. We were all sitting at the edge of the small clearing where the chestnuts made a little shade.

Then all sounds died away. At least I remember silence. Miss Robinson says that the cries of the birds were the first sign that something was happening. Far in the distance, I could hear two branches of a great chestnut tree rubbing together as the tree swayed. The rubbing noises grew shorter and shorter. Then that sound stopped also. As I looked over the green fingers of the valley, every-thing was completely still. Nothing moved. A feeling that something was about to happen came over me.

Suddenly we were all shaken by the terrible noise of Eustace's whistle. I have never heard any instrument give forth so ear-splitting a sound.

"*Please*, Eustace, dear," said Miss Mary Robinson. "You might have thought of your poor Aunt Julia's headache."

Leyland, who had been asleep, sat up.

"It is amazing how blind a boy can be to beauty," he said. "I should not have thought he could have found a way to spoil our pleasure like this."

Then the terrible silence fell upon us again. Now I was standing up, watching a stange puff of wind. Like a cat's paw, it moved down one of the ridges across from us. It turned the light green of the trees to a dark color as it traveled. A feeling that something bad was about to happen came over me. I turned away. To my surprise, I found that the others were also on their feet. They were watching the strange wind, too.

It is not possible to clearly tell what happened next. I know that the fair blue sky was above me. I know that the green spring woods were beneath me, and the kindest of friends were around me. Yet I am not ashamed to say that I became very frightened.

I was more frightened than I ever wish to become again. I was frightened in a way I never have known—either before or after. And in the eyes of the others, too, I saw fear. Their mouths moved, but they could not speak. Yet all around us was beauty and peace. And all was still— except the cat's-paw of wind now blowing up the ridge on which we stood.

Who moved first, I am not sure. It is enough to say that in one second we were all running along the hillside. Leyland was in front. Then came Sandbach, then my wife. But I only saw them for a moment. I ran across the little clearing and through the woods. I went over the rocks and down the dry creek beds into the valley below.

For all I knew, the sky might have been turning black as I ran. The hillside might have been a flat road. I saw nothing. I heard nothing. I felt nothing. All sense and reason were blocked. The fear was strong and overpowering. It was a fear that stopped up the ears, dropped clouds before the eyes, and filled the mouth with bad tastes. I ran like a frightened animal.

II

I cannot describe our finish any better than our start. Our fear passed away as it had come, without cause. But suddenly I was able to see, and hear, and cough, and clear my mouth. Looking back, I saw that the others had stopped running, too. In a short time we were all together. But it was a while before we were able to speak. It was even longer before we dared.

No one was seriously hurt. My poor wife had sprained her ankle. Leyland had torn one of his fingernails on a tree trunk. I myself had scratched my ear. I never noticed it until I stopped.

We were all silent. We looked at one another's faces. Suddenly Miss Mary Robinson gave a terrible scream. "Oh, heavens! Where is Eustace?" She would have fallen if Mr. Sandbach had not caught her.

"We must go back. We must go back at once," said my Rose. She was quite the calmest. "But I hope—I feel he is safe."

Leyland was such a coward that he tried to stay behind. But he was the only one who did. Being afraid to be left alone, he gave in. Rose and I helped my poor wife. Mr. Sandbach and Miss Robinson helped Miss Mary. Together we returned slowly. It took us 40 minutes to climb the path that we had just come down in 10 minutes.

We said little. No one wished to guess what might have happened. Rose talked the most. She surprised us all by saying that she had very nearly stayed where she was.

"Do you mean to say that you weren't—that you didn't feel a need to go?" said Mr. Sandbach.

"Oh, of course. I did feel frightened." She was the first one of us to use the word. "But I somehow felt that it would be quite different if I stayed. I was sure I wouldn't be frightened at all. And I would have stayed, I do believe," she went on, "if I had not seen Mamma go."

Rose's words made us feel a little better about Eustace. But still we had a sense that something was very wrong. We painfully climbed the chestnut-covered hills and neared the little clearing. When we reached it, we all began to talk at once. There, at the further side, was what was left of our lunch. And close by, lying very still on his back, was Eustace.

I at once cried out, "Hey, you young monkey! Jump up!" But he made no reply. He did not answer when his poor aunts spoke to him. Then, to my horror, I saw one of those green lizards run out from under his shirt.

We stood watching him as he lay there so silently. My ears began to burn as I waited for the cries of sorrow and the tears that I knew were coming.

Miss Mary fell on her knees beside him. She touched his hand where it lay in the long grass.

As she did so, he opened his eyes and smiled.

In the years since, I have often seen that strange smile. It has appeared both in person and on the pictures of him that are beginning to get into the papers. But until then, Eustace had always worn an unhappy frown. Now we were all quite surprised to see this odd smile. It seemed to show up for no reason.

His aunts rained kisses on him. He did not kiss them back. Then there was an uncomfortable pause. Eustace seemed very natural and unbothered. He did not seem the least surprised by our strange behavior. My wife tried to act as if nothing had happened.

"Well, Mr. Eustace," she said. She sat down to rest her sprained ankle. "How have you been passing the time while we were away?"

"Thank you, Mrs. Tytler, I have been very happy."

"And where have you been?"

"Here."

"And lying down all the time, you lazy boy?"

"No, not all the time."

"What were you doing before?"

"Oh, standing or sitting."

"Stood and sat doing nothing! Don't

you know the poem 'The devil finds some mischief still for idle . . .'"

"Oh, my dear madam, hush! Hush!" Mr. Sandbach's voice broke in. My wife said no more and moved away. I was surprised to see Rose take her place. In a way most unlike her, she ran her fingers through the boy's hair.

"Eustace! Eustace!" she said quickly, "tell me everything—every single thing."

Slowly he sat up. Until then he had stayed on his back, looking up at us.

"Oh, Rose . . . ," he whispered. I moved nearer to hear what he was going to say. As I did so, I noticed a few goats' footprints in the wet earth under the trees.

"It looks as if you have had a visit from some goats," I said. "I had no idea they fed up here."

Eustace got himself to his feet. He came over to take a look. When he saw the footprints, he lay down and rolled on them. He looked like a dog, rolling in dirt.

After that there was a long silence. It was broken at last by Mr. Sandbach.

"My dear friends," he said, "it is best to face the truth bravely. I know that what I am going to say is the same thing that you are all feeling. Today the Evil One has been very near us in some bodily form. Time may show us just what harm he has done to us. But at present I wish to give thanks for being saved from him."

With that, he got down on his knees. The others joined him. I got down on my knees too, though I do not believe as Sandbach does. I cannot imagine that the Devil comes among us in some form that we can see. Eustace joined in, too. He knelt quietly enough between his aunts. But when it was over, he at once got up and began hunting for something.

"Why! Someone has cut my whistle in two," he said. (I had seen Leyland with an open knife in his hand. He had pulled it out of his pocket the moment he became frightened.)

"Well, it doesn't matter," Eustace continued.

"And *why* doesn't it matter?" said Mr. Sandbach. He was hoping to trap Eustace into telling us more about that mysterious hour.

"Because I don't want it anymore."

"Why?"

At that, the boy smiled. No one seemed to have anything more to say. As fast as I could, I ran through the woods and brought up a donkey to carry my poor wife home. Nothing happened while I was gone. Rose said that she had again asked Eustace to tell her what had happened. This time he had turned away his head. He had not answered her a word.

As soon as I returned, we all set off. Eustace seemed to have a hard time walking. When we reached the other donkeys, his aunts wanted him to ride one of them home. I make it a rule never to mix in, but I put my foot down at this. As it turned out, I was perfectly right.

The healthy exercise, I suppose, began to get Eustace's blood moving. It loosened his stiff muscles. For the first time in his life, he stepped out like a man. He held his head up and took deep breaths of air into his chest. I said to Miss Mary Robinson that Eustace at last seemed to be taking some pride in his appearance. Mr. Sandbach sighed.

He said that Eustace must be carefully watched. None of us understood him yet, he explained. Miss Mary Robinson, who listened to him perhaps a bit too much, sighed too.

"Come, come, Miss Robinson," I said. "There is nothing wrong with Eustace. *Our* experiences are mysterious, not his. He was surprised when we left so suddenly. That's why he was so strange when we returned. He's all right—better than ever, if anything."

"And is this constant moving about to be counted as an improvement?" asked Leyland. He fixed a large, sad eye on Eustace. The boy had climbed upon a rock to pick some flowers. "He wants to tear from nature the few beauties that have been left to her. Is that to be counted as an improvement, too?"

It was a waste of time to answer such questions—especially when they came from an unsuccessful artist with a hurt finger. I changed the subject by asking what we should say at the hotel. It was decided that we should say nothing. We further decided to say nothing in our letters home. It took a bit of work, but I got Mr. Sandbach to agree.

Eustace did not join in our talk. We could see him racing about like a real boy in a nearby wood. A strange feeling of shame kept us from telling him about our fright. He seemed little bothered by it all. We were surprised when he ran back to us, carrying an armful of flowers.

"Do you suppose Gennaro will be there when we get back?" he called out.

Gennaro was the fill-in waiter. He was a clumsy, rude fisher boy. No one was pleased that he was taking the place of the nice, English-speaking Emmanuele. It was to Gennaro that we owed our poor lunch. I could not understand why Eustace wanted to see him. Perhaps he wanted to tell him about the strange way we had acted.

"Yes, of course he will be there," said Miss Robinson. "Why do you ask, dear?"

"Oh, I thought I would like to see him, that's all."

"And why?" snapped Mr. Sandbach.

"Because, because I do, I do. Because, because I do." He danced away into the darkening wood to the beat of his words.

"This is very strange," said Mr. Sandbach. "Did he like Gennaro before?"

"Gennaro has only been at the hotel for two days," said Rose. "They have only talked to each other a few times."

Each time Eustace returned from the wood, his spirits were higher. Once he came out screaming wildly. Another time he made believe he was a dog. The last time he came back, a poor little rabbit, too frightened to move, was sitting on his arm. The boy was getting too wild, I thought. We were all glad to leave the wood when we came to the stairs leading down to Ravello. It was late and turning dark. We hurried as fast as we could. Eustace ran in front of us like a goat.

Just where the stairs met the white road, the next strange thing of this strange day happened. Three old women were standing by the road. Like ourselves, they had come down from the woods. Heavy loads of firewood were resting on the ground beside them. Eustace stopped in front of them. After a moment's thought, he stepped forward.

He kissed one of the women on the cheek!

"My good fellow!" exclaimed Mr. Sandbach. "Are you quite mad?"

Eustace said nothing. He offered the old woman some of his flowers and then hurried on. I looked back. The old woman's friends seemed as surprised as we were. But she herself was happily holding the flowers and whispering her thanks.

We were both surprised and alarmed at the boy's strange behavior. It was no use talking to him. He either made silly replies or else ran away without answering us at all.

On the way home, Eustace said nothing more about Gennaro. I hoped that was forgotten. But when we came to the town square in front of the church, he screamed out, "Gennaro! Gennaro!" Then he began running up the little street that led to the hotel.

Sure enough, there was Gennaro at the end of the street. His long arms and legs poked out of Emmanuele's waiter's dress suit. A dirty fisherman's cap was on his head. The poor landlady always said that no matter how much she kept her eye on Gennaro, he always came to work wearing the wrong thing.

Eustace ran to meet him. He jumped right up into his arms and put his own arms around Gennaro's neck. And he did this not only in front of us. The landlady, the maid, and two American ladies who had come to stay at the hotel were also watching.

I was shocked! The boy simply could not act this way with the hired help! I took Miss Robinson aside. I asked her to let me to speak to Eustace. Someone had to tell him how to behave with those of a lower social class. She agreed. But I decided to wait until the silly boy was over all the excitement of the day. Meanwhile, Gennaro seemed to forget about taking care of the two new ladies. Instead he carried Eustace into the house. He acted as if it was the most natural thing in the world.

"*Ho capito*," I heard him say as he passed me. I knew that "*Ho capito*" is Italian for "I have understood." But Eustace had not spoken to him. I could not see what there was for Gennaro to understand. It only added to all our confusion. By the time we sat down at the table, our imaginations and our voices were worn out.

I will not describe all that was said. But for three or four hours, the seven of us went over and over all that had happened that day. Some saw a connection between the way we acted that afternoon and the way Eustace was acting now. Others saw no connection at all. Mr. Sandbach still believed that it was the work of the Devil. He also said that Eustace should see a doctor as soon as possible.

Leyland saw only a very bad boy. Rose said, to my surprise, that there must be an excuse for it all. I myself began to think that the young fellow needed a good spanking. The poor Miss Robinsons listened helplessly to all the opinions. When someone said that the boy needed a firmer hand, they agreed. When someone said he needed a gentler hand, a good beating, or a bit of medicine, they also agreed.

Dinner passed fairly well, though Eustace had trouble sitting still. As usual, Gennaro dropped knives and spoons, hawked and cleared his throat. He only knew a few words of English, so we had to use Italian to make known our wants.

Eustace, who had picked up a little of the language somewhere, asked for oranges. When Gennaro answered, he used the boy's first name and left off the "*Signor*," which is Italian for "Mister." I was shocked. This form of address is only for equals. Eustace had brought it on himself, of course. But such talk was an insult to us all. I decided to speak, and to speak at once.

When I heard Gennaro clearing the table, I went in. In Italian I said, "Gennaro! I heard you address Signor Eustace as simply 'Eustace.'"

"It is true."

"That is not right. You must be more polite. I know that Signor Eustace is sometimes silly and foolish, as he was this afternoon. Yet you must always be respectful to him. He is a young English gentleman. You are but a poor Italian fisher boy."

I know that sounds terribly snobbish. But it sounded better in Italian. Besides, it is no good speaking carefully to persons of that class. Unless you put things plainly, they act as if they don't understand you.

Gennaro only sighed and said, "It is true."

"Quite so," I said. I turned to go. Then

I heard him add, "But it is not important."

"What do you mean?" I shouted.

He came up close to me, waving his fingers.

"Signor Tytler, I wish to say something. If Eustazio asks me to call him 'Signor,' I will call him 'Signor.' Otherwise, no."

And with that, he picked up a tray of dinner things and left the room. I heard two more glasses crash to the floor.

Now I was quite angry. I marched out to talk to Eustace, but he had gone to bed. The landlady, to whom I also wished to speak, was busy. Soon we all went along to bed. It had been a most tiring and unusual day.

III

But the day was nothing to the night.

I suppose I had slept for about four hours. Then I woke up suddenly, thinking

I heard a noise in the garden. Before my eyes were even open, a cold fear took hold of me. It was not fear of something that was really happening—like the fear in the wood. This was a fear of something that *might* happen.

Our room was on the first floor. Its windows looked out onto the garden, which was covered with roses and vines and crossed with little paths. On one side stood the house. Around the two long sides ran a wall that stood only three feet above the garden. But the ground sloped down quickly. Over the wall, it was a good 20-foot drop into the olive yards on the other side.

Shaking all over, I went to the window. There, pitter-pattering up and down the paths, was something white. I was too much alarmed to see clearly. By the light of the stars, the thing took all kinds of strange shapes. At first it seemed to be a great dog, then a big bat, then a quickly moving cloud. It would bounce like a ball or fly like a bird or glide slowly like a ghost. It made no sound except for that strange *pattering*—which, after all, could only be human feet. At last I saw what it was. Eustace had gotten out of bed, and now we were in for something more.

I quickly dressed myself and went down into the dining room. The door to the garden was already unlocked. My first rush of fear had almost left me, but for five minutes I fought off a cowardly feeling. It told me not to bother the poor boy, but to watch from the window to see that he came to no harm.

At last I made myself open the door. I called out, "Eustace! What on earth are you doing? Come in at once."

He stopped pattering about. He said, "I hate my bedroom. I could not stay in it. It is too small."

"Come! Come! You never said anything about it before."

"Besides," he said, "I can't see anything—no flowers, no leaves, no sky. It only looks out on a stone wall." I knew that his view was not the best, but, as I say, he had never cared before.

"Eustace, you talk like a child!" I called out. "Come in! Do as I say quickly, if you please."

He did not move.

"Very well. I shall carry you in!" I took a few steps toward him. But I soon saw that I would never catch the boy as he ran up and down the paths. Instead, I went in to call Mr. Sandbach and Leyland to help me.

When the three of us returned, he was worse than ever. He would not even answer us when we spoke. Instead he began singing to himself in a most alarming way.

"It's a case for the doctor now," said Mr. Sandbach. He tapped his forehead.

Eustace had stopped his running. Now he was singing—first low, then loud. He sang the scales, church songs, and bits of well-known songs. His voice grew stronger and stronger. He ended with a loud shout that boomed like a gun among the mountains. It woke everyone who was still sleeping in the hotel. My poor wife and the two girls appeared at their windows. The American ladies were heard ringing their bell.

"Eustace!" we all cried. "Stop! Stop, dear boy, and come into the house."

He shook his head and started off again. This time he was talking. Never have I listened to such a strange speech. At any other time it would have been silly. Here was a boy with no idea of beauty trying to talk like the greatest of poets. Eustace Robinson, aged 14, was standing outdoors in his nightshirt. And he was speaking about the great forces of nature!

First he talked of night and the stars above his head. He spoke of the sea below, of great rivers and waterfalls, and of smoking volcanoes. He talked about the lizards that were curled up in the cracks of the earth. He talked about the white rose leaves that were caught in his hair. And then he spoke of the rain and the wind by which all things are changed. He spoke of the air through which all things live, and of the woods in which all things can be hidden.

Of course, it was all a bit much. Leyland said that it was "a devilish description of all that was most holy and beautiful in life." As usual, I felt like kicking him.

"And then," Eustace was going on, "and then there were men. But I can't make them out so well." He knelt down and rested his head on his arms.

"Now is the time," whispered Leyland. We jumped forward and tried to catch hold of him from behind. But he was away in a second. When he turned around to look at us, I could see him by the light of the stars. He was crying.

Leyland rushed at him again. We tried to corner him along the paths, but again, we had no luck.

At last, out of breath, we returned to the house. We left the boy to his madness in the far corner of the garden. Then my daughter Rose had an idea.

"Papa," she called from the window. "Go get Gennaro. He might be able to catch him for you."

I hated to ask for help from Gennaro. But I turned to the landlady who had now appeared in the garden. I asked her to call him from the coal bin where he slept.

She soon returned, followed by Gennaro. He was wearing a dress coat without either shirt or vest. He also wore a ragged pair of what once had been long pants. Now they were cut off short above the knees. The landlady, who had quite picked up English ways, scolded him for his strange dress.

"I have a coat and I have pants. What

more do you want?" Gennaro said.

"Never mind, Signora Scafetti," I put in. "As there are no ladies here, it does not matter." Then I turned to Gennaro and said, "The aunts of Mr. Eustace wish you to bring him into the house."

He did not answer.

"Do you hear me? He is not well. I order you to bring him into the house."

"Go! Go!" said Signora Scafetti. She shook him by the arm.

"Eustazio is well where he is," said Gennaro.

"Go! Go!" Signora Scafetti screamed. She let loose a flood of Italian. Most of it, I am glad to say, I could not follow. I looked up at the girls' window, but they hardly know as much Italian as I do. It is well that none of us caught one word of Gennaro's answer.

The two yelled and shouted at each other for almost ten minutes. Then Gennaro rushed back to his coal bin.

Signora Scafetti broke into tears, as well she might, for she needed her English guests.

"He says," she sobbed, "that Signor Eustace is well where he is. He says that he will not get him. I can do no more."

But *I* could. I followed Gennaro to his place of rest. In the coal bin, I found him getting comfortable under a dirty sack.

"I wish you to bring Mr. Eustace to me," I began.

He shouted something back at me that I could not understand.

"If you bring him, I will give you this." And out of my pocket I took a new ten-lire note.

This time he did not answer.

"This note is equal to ten lire in silver," I continued.

"I know it."

"That is a lot of money."

"I do not want it. Eustazio is my friend."

I put the bank-note into my pocket.

"Besides, you would not give it to me."

"I am an Englishman. The English always do what they promise."

"That is true." It is surprising how other nations trust us. Indeed, they often trust us more than we trust one another. Gennaro knelt on his sack. It was too dark to see his face. I could feel his warm breath coming out in gasps. I knew that greed had taken its hold on him.

"I could not bring Eustazio to the house. He might die there," Gennaro said at last.

"You need not do that," I answered. "You need only bring him to me. I will stand outside in the garden." And to this, as if it were something quite different, the sad young man agreed.

"But give me the ten lire first," he said.

"No." I knew the kind of person he was. I was surely not going to trust him.

We returned to the garden. Without a word, Gennaro pattered off towards the pattering that could be heard at the other end. Mr. Sandbach, Leyland, and I moved a little farther from the house. We stood in the shadow of the white climbing roses, where we could hardly be seen.

We heard the name "Eustazio" called. Then we heard silly cries of pleasure from the poor boy. The pattering stopped. We heard both of them talking. Their voices got nearer. Soon I could make out the figures of the dirty young man and the slim, white-robed boy. Gennaro had his arm around Eustace's neck. Eustace was chattering away in his quick, careless Italian.

"I understood almost everything," I heard him say. "The trees, hills, stars, water—now I can see all. But isn't it odd! I can't make out human beings a bit. Do you know what I mean?"

"*Ho capito*," said Gennaro seriously. "I have understood." He took his arm off Eustace's shoulder. Then I made the ten-lire note crackle in my pocket. Gennaro heard it. He stuck his hand out quickly, and the trusting Eustace took it in his own.

"It is strange!" Eustace went on. They were coming quite close to us now. "It almost seems as if—as if . . ."

I jumped out and caught hold of his arm. Leyland got hold of the other arm. Mr. Sandbach hung onto his feet. His screams were high and heart-shaking. The white roses were falling early that year. Both petals and leaves rained down on the boy as we pulled him into the house.

As soon as we entered the house, he stopped screaming. But tears ran silently down his face.

"Not to my room," he begged. "It is so small."

His sad look made me feel sorry for him. But what could I do? Besides, his window was the only one that had bars on it.

"Never mind, dear boy," said kind Mr.

Sandbach. "I will keep you company until the morning."

At this, he began to fight us again. "Oh, please, not that. Anything but that. I will promise to lie still and not to cry any more than I can help. Please let me be alone."

So we laid him on the bed and pulled the sheets over him. When we left him, he was crying and saying, "I nearly saw *everything*! Now I can see nothing at all."

We told the boy's aunts about all that had happened. Then we returned to the dining room. There we found Signora Scafetti and Gennaro whispering together. Mr. Sandbach got out pen and paper. He began writing a note to an English doctor. I pulled out the money at once. Then I threw the bank-note down on the table in front of Gennaro.

"Here is your pay," I said.

"Thank you very much, sir," said Gennaro. He grabbed it.

Gennaro was about to leave when

Leyland stopped him. He asked him what Eustace had meant by saying he "could not make out human beings a bit."

"I cannot say. Signor Eustazio understands many things." I was glad to hear Gennaro using "Signor" now.

"But I heard you say that you understood." Leyland kept at it.

"I do understand—but I cannot explain. I am a poor Italian fisher lad. Yet, listen. I will try." To my alarm I saw that his manner was changing. I tried to stop him. But he sat down on the edge of the table and started off. His first words were impossible to understand.

"It is sad," Gennaro said at last. "What has happened is very sad. But what can I do? I am poor. It is not I."

I turned away. Leyland went on asking questions. He wanted to know who it was that Eustace had in mind when he spoke.

"That is easy to say," Gennaro answered. "It is you. It is I. It is everyone in this house and many outside it. If he wishes for joy, we make him sad. If he asks to be alone, we bother him. He longed for a friend, but for 14 years he found none. Then he found me. But the first night, I let him down. I, who have been in the woods and understand things, too—I turn him over to you. I send him into the house to die. But what could I do?"

"Come, now," said I.

"Oh, most surely he will die. He will lie in the small room all night. In the morning he will be dead. That I know for certain."

"There! That will not do," said Mr. Sandbach. "No such thing will happen. I shall be sitting with him."

"Filomena Giusti sat all night with Caterina," Gennaro went on. "But Caterina was dead in the morning. They would not let her out. I begged and prayed. I beat the door and climbed the wall. They were fools. They thought I wished to carry her away. And in the morning she was dead."

"What is all this?" I asked Signora Scafetti.

"All kinds of stories will get about now," she replied. "And Gennaro, least of anyone, has reason to spread them."

"I am alive now," Gennaro went on, "only because I had neither parents nor friends. When the first night came, I could run through the woods and climb the rocks and dive into the water. But then I found what I really wanted."

We heard a cry from Eustace's room. It was a soft but steady sound, like the wail of wind in a far-off wood.

"That," said Gennaro, "was the last noise Caterina made. I was hanging onto her window then. I heard it clearly."

He lifted up his hand. I could see my ten-lire note in it. He shouted angry words at Mr. Sandbach, and Leyland,

and myself. He shouted at Fate because Eustace was dying in the upstairs room. Just then the fool Leyland turned over the lamp with his elbow. Since it was a lamp made to go out if it fell over, the light went out. The change from light to dark had great power over Gennaro, just as it would over an animal.

I felt, rather than saw, that he had left the room. I shouted out to Mr. Sandbach, "Have you got the key to Eustace's room?" But Mr. Sandbach and Leyland were both on the floor. Each man had thought the other was Gennaro. More time was wasted in finding a match. Mr. Sandbach said that he had left the key in the door—in case the Miss Robinsons wished to pay Eustace a visit. Then we all turned as we heard a noise. There was Gennaro, carrying Eustace down the stairs.

We rushed out and blocked the hall. At that, Gennaro turned and carried

Eustace back to the upstairs landing.

"Now they are caught!" cried Signora Scafetti. "There is no other way out."

We were carefully climbing the stairs when there was a scream from my wife's room. The scream was followed by a heavy thud on the path. The boys had jumped out of her window!

I reached the garden just in time to see Eustace jumping over the garden wall. This time I knew for certain that he would be killed. But he landed in an olive tree. There he looked like a great white moth. I watched as he slowly slid down from the tree. As soon as his bare feet touched the ground, he gave a strange loud cry. I would not have thought the human voice could have made such a sound. Then he disappeared among the trees.

"He has understood, and he is saved," cried Gennaro. He was sitting on the wall. "Now instead of dying he will live!"

"And you, instead of keeping the ten lire, will give it up," I exclaimed.

"The money is mine," he hissed back in a whisper. He held the bank-note to his chest to protect it. As he did so, he swayed forward and fell upon his face on the path. He had not broken any bones. A fall like that would never have killed an Englishman, for the drop was not great. But something had gone wrong inside Gennaro, and he was dead.

Morning was still far off, but the morning breeze had come up. More white rose petals fell on us as we carried him in. Signora Scafetti began screaming at the sight of the dead body. And we could hear something else from far down the valley. On towards the sea, there still sounded the shouts and the laughter of the escaping boy.

The Other Side of the Hedge

Have you ever imagined what heaven might be like? In this thoughtful story, the main character actually visits "the other side." As you read, look for the insights behind the author's imagination.

On this side, the hedge was green instead of brown.

The Other Side
of the Hedge

My pedometer measured how far I had come. By counting my steps, the clever little machine told me that I was 25. I know it is a shocking thing to stop walking. But I was very tired. So I sat down to rest on a milestone.

People went past, laughing at me as they did so. But I didn't care enough to feel angry. Miss Eliza Dimbleby, one of the world's great teachers, hurried past. She called to me to "keep at it" and "never give up." I only smiled at her and raised my hat.

At first I thought I was going to be like my brother. I had had to leave him by the roadside a year or two ago. He had wasted his breath on singing. His strength was used up on helping others. But I had been wiser. Now it was only the boredom of the road that bothered me. Every mile was the same—nothing but dust under foot and brown crackling hedges on either side. It had been the same ever since I could remember.

To lighten my load, I had already dropped several things along the way. Indeed, the road behind was dotted with the things we all had dropped. The white dust was settling down on them. Already they looked no different than stones.

My muscles were tired. Now I could not even bear the weight of those things I still carried. I slid off the milestone into the road. I lay there flat out, with my face turned to the great, dry hedge. I prayed that I might give up.

A little puff of air brought me around. It seemed to come from the hedge. When I opened my eyes, I saw a bit of light coming through the branches and dead leaves. The hedge could not be as thick as usual. In my weak, gloomy state, I longed to force my way in. I wanted to see what was on the other side. No one was in sight, or I should not have dared to try. We of the road do not admit that there is another side at all.

I gave in. I said to myself that I would come back to the road in a minute. The thorns scratched my face, and I had to use my arms to protect myself. I used my feet alone to push me forward. Halfway through, I thought about going back. Inside the hedge, all the things that I was carrying were scraped off of me. My clothes were torn, too. But I was boxed in! Since return was impossible, I had to crawl blindly forward. I was afraid that my strength was going to give out. Now

I felt sure that I would die inside the hedge.

Suddenly cold water closed around my head. I seemed to be sinking down forever. I had fallen out of the hedge into a deep pool. I rose to the top at last, crying for help. I heard someone on the bank laugh and say, "Another!" Then I was pulled out and laid gasping on the dry ground.

Even when the water was out of my eyes, nothing seemed clear. I had never been in so large a space. I had never seen such grass and sunshine. The blue sky was no longer a strip. Under the sky, the earth had risen into clean, bare hills. There were beech trees on the hillsides and meadows and clear pools all around. There was a feeling of human life in the place. One might have called it a park or a garden—but those words were too simple and plain.

I got my breath. Then I turned to the

fellow who had saved me. "Where does this place lead to?" I asked.

"Nowhere, thank the Lord!" he said with a laugh. I saw that he looked to be a man of 50 or 60—too old for the road. But there was no worry nor hurry in his manner, and his voice was as clear as a boy's.

"But it must lead somewhere!" I cried. I was too surprised at his answer to thank him for saving my life.

"He wants to know where it leads!" he shouted to some men on the hill. They laughed back and waved their caps.

I noticed then that the pool into which I had fallen was really a moat. It circled around to the left and to the right. The hedge followed it all the way. On this side, the hedge was green instead of brown. Its roots showed through the clear water, and fish swam about in them. Flowering vines grew over the hedge.

But then I saw that it was a fence of sorts—a barrier. In a moment I lost all pleasure in the place. I no longer enjoyed the grass, the sky, the trees, the happy men and women. I realized that it was nothing but a prison, no matter how big or beautiful.

We moved away from the hedge. Then we followed a path across the meadows. I found it hard walking, for I was always trying to go faster than my guide. It was silly, for there was no reason to hurry if the place led nowhere. But I had not kept step with anyone since I left my brother. I had forgotten how.

I made the fellow smile by stopping suddenly and saying unhappily, "This is perfectly terrible. I cannot move forward here. I cannot get ahead. Now, we of the road—"

"Yes. I know."

"I was going to say, we are always moving forward."

"I know."

"We are always learning, getting better, changing. Why, even in my short life I have seen a great deal of change. Science, governments, religion, and education are always changing. Here, for example—"

I took out my pedometer and saw that it still marked only 25, and not a bit more.

"Oh, it's stopped," I said. "I wanted to show you. The pedometer should have recorded all the time that I've been walking with you. But it still makes me no more than 25."

"Many things from the other side don't work in here," he said.

"The laws of science are the same anywhere in the world," I protested. "It must be the water in the moat that has hurt the machinery. If things are normal, then everything works. Science and the drive to do better all the time—those are the forces that have made us what we are!"

I had to break off then and return the pleasant hellos of people we were passing. Some of them were singing. Some were talking. And others were gardening, cutting hay, or doing some other simple job. They all seemed happy. I might have been happy too, if I could have forgotten that the place led to nowhere.

I was surprised by a young man who came running across our path. He jumped a little fence in fine style. Then he went tearing across a field and dove into a lake. He began to swim across it. Here was true energy, I thought. "A cross-country race!" I exclaimed. "Where are the others?"

"Why, there are no others," my guide replied. Later on we passed some long grass. From behind the grass we heard the voice of a girl. She was singing most beautifully to herself. Again he said, "There are no others." I was confused at the waste of talent. "What does it all mean?"

He said, "It means nothing but itself." Then he repeated the words slowly, as if I were a child.

"I understand," I said quietly. "But I do not agree. What we do is worth nothing unless it is a link in the chain of progress. And I must not accept your kindness any longer. Somehow I must get back to the road. And I must have my pedometer fixed."

"First, you must see the gates," the man replied. "We do have gates, though we never use them."

Just to be nice, I gave in. Before long we reached the moat again. At this point, a white bridge crossed over it. The gate opened outwards and led to a road. I exclaimed in surprise, for it was just such a road as I had left. It was dusty under foot, with brown crackling hedges on either side as far as the eye could see.

"That's my road!" I cried.

He shut the gate and said, "But not *your part* of the road. It is through this gate that humankind went out ages ago. That was when humans were first overcome with the desire to walk."

I shook my head at this. I knew that the part of the road I had left was no more than two miles off. But nothing could change his mind. He repeated, "It is the same road. This is the beginning. Though it seems to run straight away from us, the road doubles back every so often. It is never far from our boundary. Sometimes the road even touches it."

Then the old fellow got on his knees by the moat. On the wet ground he drew a strange figure like a maze. As we walked back through the meadows, I tried to make him see his mistake.

"The road *sometimes* doubles back, to

be sure," I explained. "But that is part of our way. Who can doubt that most movement is forward? To what goal, we know not. It may be to some mountain where we shall touch the sky. It may be into the sea. But the road *does* go forward. Who can doubt that? It is the thought of going forward that makes us work to be our best—each in his own way. It gives us the push that you people here do not seem to have.

"Think about that man who passed us. It is true that he ran well, and jumped well, and swam well. But look on the other side of the hedge! We have men who can run better, and men who can jump better, and men who can swim better. People have worked hard to become best at just one thing. They specialize. The results of specializing would surprise you. Just so, that girl—"

Here I stopped myself. "Good heavens!" I exclaimed. "I could have sworn it was

Miss Eliza Dimbleby over there. Look there at that woman with her feet in the fountain!"

He said he believed that it was.

"Impossible! I left her on the road. She is going to speak before a crowd this evening at Tunbridge Wells. Why, her train leaves Cannon Street in . . . Of course! My watch has stopped like everything else. She is the last person I would expect to be here."

"People always are surprised at meeting each other here. But all kinds come through the hedge. And they come at all times—when they are drawing ahead in the race, when they are falling behind, when they are left for dead.

"I often stand near the boundary, listening to the sounds of the road. You know what they are. And I wonder if anyone will turn aside. It makes me very happy to help someone out of the moat, as I helped you. Our country fills up slowly, though it was meant for all mankind."

"Human beings have other aims," I said gently, for I thought that he meant well. "And I must join them." I told him good evening, for the sun was going down. I wished to be on the road by the time night fell. To my alarm, he caught hold of me. "You are not to go yet!" he cried. I tried to shake him off. Really, we had nothing in common, and he was beginning to bother me. But for all my pulling away, the old man would not let go. As wrestling is not my specialty, I had to follow him.

Alone, I could have never found the place where I came in. My hope was that he would take me back when I had seen the other sights. I was sure of only one thing: I did not want to sleep in this country. I did not trust it, nor the people either, even though they seemed friendly. Hungry though I was, I would not join them in their suppers of milk and fruit. When they gave me flowers, I threw them all away as soon as no one was watching.

Already these people were getting ready for the night, lying down like cows. Some were out on the bare hillside. Others were in groups under the beech trees. In the light of an orange sunset, I hurried on with my guide. I was dead tired and weak for want of food. But I kept whispering, "Give me life, with all its struggles. Give me life, with its wins and its losses. Give me life with its deep meaning and its unknown goal!"

At last we came to a place where another bridge crossed the moat. I saw that another gate broke the line of the boundary hedge. It was different from the first gate. I could see through parts of it like glass, and it opened inwards. But through that gate, in the last light of the day, I saw again just such a road as I had left. It was a dusty road with brown crackling hedges on either side as far as the eye could see.

I was strangely bothered by the sight. I felt that I had lost all control. A man was passing us, returning to the hills for the night. He had a long rake over his shoulder and a can of some kind of drink in his hand. Somehow I forgot the questions of mankind. I forgot the road that lay before my eyes. Now I sprang at him, pulled the can out of his hand, and began to drink.

It was nothing stronger than beer, but in my tired state it overcame me quickly. As in a dream, I saw the old man shut the gate. I heard him say, "This is where your road ends. Through this gate, humankind—all that is left of it—will come to us."

Though my senses were sinking into nothingness, for a brief moment they seemed to become sharper. I heard the magic song of the night birds. I smelled the hay. I saw the bright stars in the darkening sky. The man whose beer I had taken lowered me down gently to sleep. As he did so, I saw that he was my brother.

Thinking About
the Stories

The Story of a Panic

1. All the events in a story are arranged in a certain order, or sequence. Tell about one event from the beginning of this story, one from the middle, and one from the end. How are these events related?

2. Suppose this story had a completely different outcome. Can you think of another effective ending for this story?

3. Did the story plot change direction at any point? Explain the turning point of the story.

The Other Side of the Hedge

1. Good writing always has an effect on the reader. How did you feel when you finished reading this story? Were you surprised, horrified, amused, sad, touched, or inspired? What elements in the story made you feel that way?

2. Compare and contrast at least two characters in this story. In what ways are they alike? In what ways are they different?

3. All stories fit into one or more categories. Is this story serious or funny? Would you call it an adventure, a love story, or a mystery? Is it a character study? Or is it simply a picture the author has painted of a certain time and place? Explain your thinking.